From Hero to Zero to Freedom

How Losing Myself Through Duty, Betrayal, and Blind Faith Led Me to Spiritual Awakening

DT Comer

From Hero to Zero to Freedom
DT Comer

Copyright © 2025 DT Comer. All Rights reserved.

No part of this publication may be reproduced, distributed, or transmitted in any form or by any means, including photocopying, recording, or other electronic or mechanical methods, without the prior written permission of the author, except in the case of brief quotations embodied in critical reviews and certain other non-commercial uses permitted by copyright law. For permission requests, please contact the author directly at:

DT Comer
Email: dtcomer@gmail.com
ISBN: 978-0-9767408-8-9

Author Introduction
Why I Wrote *From Hero to Zero to Freedom*

People often ask me, "Why did you write this book?" or "Why call it *From Hero to Zero to Freedom?*"

For me, this book is about what happens when you think you're on top of the world—everything's working, life is steady, and you believe your foundation is solid—and then one day, it all collapses. Everything you believed, everything you trusted, everything you thought you understood about life, faith, and yourself just doesn't hold up anymore.

You start asking questions you never thought you'd have to ask: *Was I duped? Why didn't I see this coming? What was really going on?*

That's when I began to realize—this was all about the foundation.

From childhood, through school, through the people who shaped us—teachers, friends, family—we're all laying bricks in what becomes our foundation. And that foundation determines how we handle life's storms, its controversies, and its hard knocks.

But here's the truth I discovered: the foundation matters.

See, I thought mine was solid. I believed it was built with rock, or maybe concrete—something strong and unshakable. But what I learned was that my foundation wasn't made of rock at all. It was made of **ice.**

Think about that. Ice feels solid—until it melts.

If your foundation is built on ice, you have to treat it differently. You can't wear heated boots. You can't stand in one place too long. You have to move with care because what supports you is fragile, temporary, and can shift without warning.

For years, I was walking confidently on that ice—believing it was rock—until one day it cracked. Everything I'd built on top of it—my beliefs, my identity, my relationships, my sense of control—started to sink.

That's when I realized: it was never as solid as I thought.

And that's why I wrote this book. To talk about the difference between a foundation that's truly solid and one that only *appears* to be. To explore what happens when you finally face the cracks beneath your own feet—and to show that even when the ice gives way, you can rebuild.

Because not all foundations are the same. Some can be strengthened. Some lose their strength over time. And sometimes, freedom begins the moment you stop pretending your ice is rock.

Contents

Author Introduction IV

Introduction 1

Chapter 1 - Campfire and Commandments 5

Chapter 2 - Sunday School and the Sound of Fear 9

Chapter 3 - Saints, Sins, and Silence 11

Chapter 4 - Who Ya Rootin' For 19

Chapter 5 - War, Women, and Worship 25

Chapter 6 - The House We Didn't Build 37

Chapter 7 - Yes-Yallin' and the Therapist Who Called It Out ... 45

Chapter 8 - Power Plays and Passovers 53

Chapter 9 - The Return to Self 61

Chapter 10 - Learning to Love Without Losing Yourself 65

Chapter 11 - Lov**ing** Without Losing: **Choosing Peace** 71

Chapter 12 - Rewriting the Rules 77

Chapter 13 - Redemption Is a Quiet Thing 83

Chapter 14 - The Choice 89

Epilogue - The Wake-Up Call 93

Introduction

Why I'm Writing This Now

I'm writing this book now because I've been carrying emotional pain for most of my life—some of it I've understood, but much of it has gone unnamed and unexplored. That pain stems from childhood experiences and belief systems that were handed to me without question, absorbed like gospel, and reinforced by the environments I grew up in. For decades, I lived in those beliefs. I served within them. I made decisions and sacrifices by them. I never thought to challenge them—until they broke me.

Now, as I enter my 60s, I feel compelled to speak honestly about what I've discovered—not just about my life, but about my faith. I've been humbled by loss, betrayal, disappointment, and silence. And through it all, I've had to ask myself: *What do I actually believe? Who told me what God wants from me? And why did I spend so much of my life trying to be good by someone else's standard?*

Who This Book Is For

This book is for people who've outgrown the faith they were raised in—but don't know what to believe anymore. It's for those who appear successful on the outside but feel disconnected on the inside. It's for those who have given all they could to others, to systems, to communities, only to be left behind, unseen, or betrayed.

If you've ever felt like doing "the right thing" keeps costing you your peace, your identity, and your voice—this book is for you. If you've ever followed all the rules and still ended up feeling empty, you're not alone. And if you've ever wondered whether there's still something better waiting for you, even after it all fell apart—I'm here to say: there is.

Why Obedience Failed Me

Obedience didn't fail me because obedience is wrong—it failed me because mine was blind. I was trained in systems that rewarded compliance. I was taught to follow orders, not question them. That mindset didn't stay in the Army—it followed me into marriage, into faith, into leadership, and into how I saw myself.

I made choices based not on inner clarity but on outer expectation. I trusted people and processes that didn't earn that trust. I ignored my instincts—the same instincts that kept me alive in combat. I overrode what I felt in my spirit because I believed God would honor my sacrifice if I just kept being faithful. But what I learned—through heartbreak and silence—is that *faith without discernment is a trap.*

Why Freedom Started with Honesty

My journey to freedom didn't start with success, or healing, or even forgiveness. It started with honesty. Honesty about who I really was—not who I was told to be, not who I tried to become for others, and not who I pretended to be when I didn't know better.

Therapy helped me peel back the layers. Self-reflection forced me to ask new questions. Who am I to myself? Who am I to my family, my friends, my God? What patterns did I inherit that are no longer mine to carry? Only when I began answering those questions—with raw, sometimes uncomfortable truth—did I start to feel free.

This book is a mirror. It's not a guide. It's not a sermon. It's a reflection of one man who tried his best to follow the rules—and finally realized he had to break them to become whole.

Chapter 1

Campfire and Commandments

I remember it like it was yesterday. Yes, I can see the elementary school version of me—sitting in front of the TV on a Saturday or Sunday evening leading up to Easter.

There we were, glued to the screen, watching *The Ten Commandments* with Charlton Heston playing Moses.

And there it was:

God Himself, etching commandments into stone with fire—while Moses shielded his eyes from the glory of it.

That scene?

It burned into my memory.

So when it came to going to church and all things Sunday School, that was the foundation.

The Ten Commandments weren't suggestions.

They were orders.

Directives.

No ambiguity. No debate.

Break one—just one—and it was a one-way ticket to Hell.

Do not pass GO. Do not collect two hundred dollars. Straight down.

That's how I absorbed religion as a child.

It wasn't about relationship.

It was about rules.

We didn't talk much about grace.

We didn't ask why we had to go to church.

You went—because bad things happen to people who don't.

No one ever sat me down to say that bad things happen all the time—for reasons that have nothing to do with missing Sunday School.

But that nuance? It never made it into the sermons.

One of the earliest, most vivid church memories I have isn't from a chapel—but from a Christian camp retreat.

It was the first time I'd ever been away from home.

I was just a kid.

The military Protestant church took us Sunday School kids out for four days of Jesus, nature, and s'mores.

We picnicked.

Told ghost stories around the campfire.

Had Bible study.

Attended devotionals.

Sang songs.

Took communion.

It was fun.

It was peaceful.

And it made being a Christian feel like belonging.

I was shown that being around other God-fearing people could be joyful. That community could be holy. That maybe—just maybe—there was more to church than fear.

I believed that if I stayed close to Godly people, I'd be safe.

That all church people were good people.

It was something I believed for far too long.

Chapter 2

Sunday School and the Sound of Fear

It didn't matter which base we lived on or which chapel we attended—Sunday School was always the same: a classroom filled with military kids like me, coloring pages of David and Goliath, and a constant warning humming beneath every lesson—*don't mess up or God will make you pay.*

I loved the story of Samson and Delilah, though I probably didn't understand half of the nuances at the time. I just knew this man had strength beyond belief, and he lost it because he trusted the wrong woman. She betrayed him, sold him out. She got him captured which left him weak, blind, and broken. Even as a kid, I got that part. And when Samson cried out to God—pissed off and heartbroken—I felt it.

Just like that, he became a pawn – and she walked away. Samson cried out to God. "Why would You let this happen to me?" Wasn't Samson loyal? Samson was strong. He was Chosen. He had a divine purpose. But even he got played. And it wasn't his enemies that broke him-it was the person he trusted most. That hit a little to close, even as a kid.

That question stuck with me. Still does.

Sunday School didn't offer answers, just fear. If you break the rules, if you question the system, if you step out of line—there's a consequence. End of story.

And yet, every week we showed up. Sat in pews. Folded our hands. Repeated memory verses like we were in boot camp for Heaven.

Nobody explained why we went to church. We just went. Nobody said, "God loves you." They said, "God's watching." Nobody taught me grace. They taught me guilt.

So when I skipped out on Sunday School to hang in the park or walk home instead of staying for service, it wasn't rebellion. It was relief. Even back then, I was quietly pushing back. Not against God—but against the weight of religion. The suffocating performance of it all. There's something that happens when your early relationship with God is built on punishment instead of love. You internalize the idea that being good is a performance. That salvation was conditional. If you mess up, you better brace for impact. So we followed the rules. Or at least tried. We prayed out of guilt. We repented out of fear. And we obeyed-because we were told bad things would happen if we didn't. That kind of theology doesn't just shape your behavior. It shapes your identity. It makes you cautious with your emotions. Paranoid with your decisions. Rigid with your beliefs. Because if God is mostly wrath and disappointment, how do you ever feel worthy of love?

That was the blueprint I was given: God as judge, church as courtroom, and me always on trial.

And that blueprint followed me.

For years.

Long after I stopped coloring inside the lines.

Chapter 3

Saints, Sins, and Silence

I didn't grow up Catholic. But from the moment I walked into that private Catholic boys school at thirteen years old, I realized that not being Catholic was going to be the least of the things that made me different.

I was one of only a handful of African American students in the entire school.

I'd been raised in a military household—disciplined, dutiful, and expected to make no excuses.

We moved where we were told.

We worshipped in Protestant chapels on base where God was taught as a strict but fair commander.

You followed the commandments.

You didn't question the rules.

You prayed, you obeyed, and you feared falling out of line.

So stepping into the ornate, hushed world of Catholicism felt like being dropped into a different country altogether.

The first thing I noticed was the rituals—the kneeling, the genuflecting, the holy water, the stained glass depictions of saints with halos and sorrowful eyes.

Everyone around me moved through it all like it was second nature.

Meanwhile, I stood out. Not just because of my skin or my background, but because I didn't understand why any of it mattered.

I remember asking early on, "Why do we pray to Mary?"

The answer came quickly, like it had been memorized: "We don't pray to her. We ask her to intercede on our behalf."

But to me, that felt like semantics. Where I came from, there was one God. One Son. One direct line. Anything else—saints, icons, intermediaries—felt like stepping into forbidden territory.

I'd been taught that *"Thou shall have no other gods before me"* wasn't just a rule—it was the rule.

It didn't help that the priests seemed distant, untouchable.

They didn't just teach us—they *instructed* us with the authority of someone who could not be questioned.

Their robes, their tones, even the way they moved felt detached from real life.

I respected the formality, but I didn't trust it.

Where was the warmth?

Where was the relationship?

Where was God?

Confession, in particular, left me twisted inside. The idea of sitting in a booth and telling a stranger my sins so they could grant me absolution? That felt wrong like was the sin going away?

I'd been taught to go straight to God with my wrongs. No middleman. No performance. No counting out Hail Marys like spiritual currency to buy forgiveness.

And yet, at school, this wasn't just encouraged—it was expected.

I found myself watching my classmates confess and then exit like they'd unloaded something heavy.

Meanwhile, I carried my questions in silence, unsure who I could even ask.

Because challenging doctrine didn't feel like curiosity here.

It felt like defiance.

And maybe that was the most damaging part of those years—not the theology, but the quiet.

The way I learned to swallow my doubt and wear a respectful mask.

But here's the truth:

I didn't lose my belief in God.

I just stopped believing anyone else knew how to explain Him.

What I was being taught at school clashed so violently with what I'd absorbed as a child that I didn't shut down—I fought back.

I questioned everything.

I poked holes in their doctrine, challenged their rituals, and openly ridiculed what felt like spiritual theater.

No one could give me a straight answer that made sense.

And frankly, I wasn't convinced anyone truly believed the things they were doing either.

I remember thinking:

My God doesn't need all this pomp and circumstance.

My God doesn't need intermediaries.

I believed in a direct connection.

No saints.

No confession booths.

No recitations on loop like some kind of magic spell.

Just me and God. That was enough.

And I didn't keep those thoughts to myself.

I became an annoyance—I knew it. And I didn't care.

The more I saw people around me practicing ritual without depth, the more convinced I became that much of what I was witnessing wasn't authentic.

It was mechanical.

Performed.

Empty.

The term *"practicing Catholic"* started to sound like a joke.

I'd hear classmates or even teachers say, "Well, I'm Catholic… but I'm not practicing."

And I'd think: Then what are you?

The contradiction irritated me.

To me, religion wasn't something you could dip in and out of when it was convenient.

Either you were in or you weren't.

I didn't see Catholicism as a better or deeper faith.

I saw it as a religion wrapped in tradition, hierarchy, and cultural guilt—but not spiritual connection.

And I pushed back hard.

Years later, I'd come to understand that many people carry their religion like inherited furniture—too sacred to throw out, too uncomfortable to live with.

But back then, I had no such patience.

I wanted truth.

And if I couldn't find it in the rituals, I had no use for them.

But nothing solidified my slow burn toward the Church—and, if I'm honest, toward God Himself—like what happened that day in the locker room.

It was just a normal day after gym. I had forgotten a book and ran back into the locker room to grab it.

I wasn't expecting anyone else to be there—but I walked in and caught a classmate red-handed, going through someone else's wallet.

He saw me. I saw him.

And he knew the deal.

Before I could even open my mouth, he offered me a deal:

"I'll split it with you. Just don't say anything."

I didn't steal the money.

I didn't touch the wallet.

But I didn't say no either.

It wasn't my business, I told myself.

I didn't put my hands on anything.

And in my world, being a snitch got you far worse than staying silent.

So I didn't say a word.

But the universe—or God, or karma, or just bad luck—wasn't done with us.

Later that day, someone found the wallet and turned it in.

Empty, of course.

And it didn't take the Christian Brothers long to narrow it down to the class we were both in.

That's when the spiritual chastising began—heavy-handed, sermon-like lectures meant to guilt someone into confession.

I remember sitting there stone-faced, quiet.

I didn't steal it. That was the truth.

But I didn't speak up either.

And I had my reasons.

Eventually, the pressure cracked the thief.

He came clean and was pulled out of class.

I thought that was the end of it.

It wasn't.

Maybe thirty minutes later, I was summoned out of class.

And just like that, I knew—he had told them I knew.

Of course he had. Misery loves company. If he was going down, he wasn't going alone.

But here's where things got real twisted.

He got forgiveness.

After confession and a round of Hail Marys, he was welcomed back with open arms.

His soul had been "cleansed."

His guilt washed away.

Me?

I was suspended.

Not for stealing.

Not for lying.

But for not telling.

And I couldn't help but wonder:

Was it because I didn't confess—or because I wasn't Catholic?

Or worse… was it because I was Black?

That moment did something to me.

I was livid—not just at the school, not just at the Christian Brothers, but at the entire institution of religion.

How could a system that claimed to be based on justice and mercy be this hypocritical?

How could God—if He was even watching—let this be the outcome?

I didn't commit a sin by Catholic standards, but I also didn't have the right spiritual credentials to earn their version of forgiveness.

That was the beginning of my spiritual fracture.

The first time I felt the cold hand of religious injustice not just as an observer, but as the one being judged by it.

From that moment forward, I wasn't just questioning.

I was done playing along.

And deep inside, something started to shift—not just in how I saw the Church, but in how I saw God.

If He was real,

He had some explaining to do.

Chapter 4

Who Ya Rootin' For

"Who ya rootin' for... P-V-U? Who ya rootin' for... P-V-U?"

Man, those HBCU homecoming chants are permanently etched in my soul. From the Labor Day Classic between Prairie View A&M and Texas Southern,

to the State Fair Classic against Grambling State,

to every wild halftime show in between...

You can't fake the funk on HBCU tradition.

The students. The alumni. The band. The tailgates. The chants.

The Blackness. The pride.

It was a vibe—and for me, it was a cultural reset.

As they say down south—and in most Black churches before any gathering, big or small:

"And the glory be to GOD."

At Prairie View, God wasn't confined to a pulpit.

He was in the music.

He was in the drumline.

He was in the way we danced, the way we studied, the way we showed up for one another.

Spirituality wasn't rigid here—it was alive.

And while I wasn't fully aware of it at the time, something inside me was beginning to shift.

The black-and-white religious mindset I carried from my childhood?

It started to bleed into color again.

Attending school in the country had its perks.

When you're isolated, **belonging** becomes a kind of currency.

Nobody wanted to be a G.D.I.—a "God-Damned Independent."

That was just code for, *You don't belong anywhere.*

Not me, baby.

This country kid from El Paso, Texas—with a slightly Spanish accent and a military background—came in with credentials.

I was the only freshman in my class with a four-year Army ROTC scholarship.

I didn't know my left face from my right yet, but it didn't matter.

I was **somebody.**

ROTC gave me identity.

It gave me brothers and sisters.

It gave me purpose.

And to solidify that commitment, I pledged **Pershing Rifles (P/R)** my freshman year—a military fraternity.

I'm not about to go into all the extra that goes into pledging a military frat, in the South, at an HBCU.

If you know… you know.

Let's just say I was spinning rifles, tossing them across drill lines, marching in parades, and showing out at competitions like I was born to do it.

And yet, somewhere in between drills and dorm rooms,

something else started happening…

I started finding **God** again.

Not in rules.

Not in robes.

Not in recited Hail Marys.

But in *real-life* spaces.

In conversations.

In quiet moments.

I found myself going to chapel on Sundays.

Riding off campus to attend church in Houston with friends.

Visiting churches with girlfriends.

Experiencing *different* kinds of praise.

More joy. More color. More presence.

This time, there was no guilt.

No shame.

No empty rituals.

I wasn't faking it.

I wasn't pretending.

I wasn't being told who God was.

I was starting to feel who God might actually be—for myself.

And for the first time since that childhood campfire retreat,

church felt good again.

And just when things were leveling out spiritually...

Came another pivotal moment:

Spring semester, sophomore year.

I made line for **Kappa Alpha Psi.**

Now that was real business.

If you know anything about Black Greek life,

you know the "Pretty Boyz" don't play.

Getting on line was no small feat—especially with 100+ men showing up at the Smoker.

But I made it.

And pledging Kappa?

Whew.

That took *faith*.

Real faith.

Faith in myself.

Faith in my line brothers.

Faith that I was being molded into something deeper.

We prayed.

We sweat.

We shouted.

We leaned on God a lot during that process.

And when we crossed?

It wasn't just the end of a line.

It was the beginning of me reclaiming my spiritual self.

Chapter 5

War, Women, and Worship

Part I: Adultery on the Road

I was still new in my role—young, sharp, and maybe a little too idealistic. My first road mission as a platoon leader was a multi-day trip from **Fort Lewis, Washington** to **Fort Hunter Liggett, California**. It was our job to convoy heavy equipment and vehicles. We moved in formation, stopped on schedule, and conducted load checks like clockwork.

We weren't even two hours into the journey before the masks came off.

At our very first rest stop, I saw it:

Married soldiers making plans—casual like it was nothing.

They had rendezvous points already set up. Women in other towns. Hotels. Code words.

I was shocked.

And I asked, "Why even get married if you're gonna do this?"

One of the enlisted soldiers—older than me—grinned and said:

"Sir… sometimes you get tired of the same ol' steak and potatoes."

That answer sat in my gut like a stone.

All my life, I had been taught that adultery was one of the Big Ones.

A Commandment you don't break.

Not without serious consequence.

But these men weren't worried about judgment.

They weren't afraid of divine punishment.

They were just... living.

It was my first real **disillusionment**.

The Bible had trained me to believe that sin was followed by wrath.

But here, sin looked casual. Boring, even.

And wrath? Nowhere in sight.

I started to ask myself questions I didn't have answers to:
- Was God watching this?
- Was this normal and I'd just been naive?
- Had I misunderstood everything about morality?

This wasn't a philosophical moment.

This was a *spiritual fracture*.

The kind of moment that lingers—long after the convoy ends.

Part II: God in the Crossfire

Coming home from the war should've been a moment of celebration. And in many ways, it was. I brought my soldiers back alive. I led during combat, held the line, made calls I wasn't ready for—but I did it. I was proud of that. Proud of them. Proud of myself.

But something in me had shifted. I couldn't explain it. It was like the version of me who went overseas didn't make it back. My body returned. My smile returned. But my spirit? That was still somewhere in the desert, staring down the ruins of someone else's life.

Not long after I got back, I met my first wife at the Officer Advanced Course. We connected quickly. Looking back now, it wasn't love. It was velocity. We were both professionals, both with goals. And I think I was just ready to do something that felt normal. Something that felt like progress. Like a future.

We eloped. Just like that. No deep conversations, no big plans. We agreed to live apart for a year because of our assignments, but even then—I should've known.

That year apart was a test we never studied for.

I started noticing how women looked at me differently after I got married. Not with respect, but with curiosity. Like I was suddenly a challenge. Forbidden fruit. It was strange—and if I'm being honest, it was flattering. It made me feel wanted, desired, validated.

I didn't cheat. But I thought about it. A lot.

And that's when I realized: I didn't really know what marriage was. I knew how to lead soldiers. I knew how to survive war. But I didn't know how to be vulnerable. I didn't know how to open up. I didn't know how to be married.

Twelve months later, we were divorced.

And just like that, another belief crumbled. I used to think that doing the right thing was enough. That if you chose marriage, chose commitment, chose church—you'd be rewarded with peace, love, or at least stability.

But that wasn't how it worked.

Right around that time, I got introduced to the Apostolic Church. And let me tell you—if you've never been to an Apostolic service, it's an experience. The shouting, the dancing, the speaking in tongues. The spirit would come over people like a storm. And sometimes it came over me, too.

But I wasn't just attending those services—I was orchestrating them.

I was learning to play the bass guitar at the time, and before long, I found myself on stage, fingers plucking the groove that would set the whole sanctuary on fire. I watched for the signs—the moment the preacher started getting "happy," when his voice cracked with passion and his feet started moving. That's when I'd take the lead.

I'd lay down a riff. The drummer would catch it. The organist would swell. And just like that, the whole place would erupt.

People shouting. People running. People crying. It was electric.

And I felt it. I really did. For a while, I thought I was finally plugged into something holy, something transcendent. I wasn't just in the building—I was moving the spirit.

It felt powerful. It felt divine.

And for a time, I convinced myself it was divine.

But here's what I didn't understand then:

Emotion isn't the same as transformation.

Performance isn't the same as healing.

And noise isn't the same as truth.

Looking back, I realize I wasn't just playing bass—I was playing a part. I was helping people feel something we all desperately needed to feel… but maybe not something we truly understood.

I was trying to fill a crater with shouting. Trying to drown my doubts in crescendos and chord progressions. Trying to sweat out my pain through other people's hallelujahs.

And when the music stopped?

The silence was deafening.

Because all the questions were still there. All the pain was still there. All the confusion and heartbreak and self-betrayal—it never left.

That was the start of me questioning not just my faith, but my understanding of faith.

Because if God was in all this—why did I still feel so empty?

Why did I feel lonelier in church than I ever did in the field?

Why did I keep doing "the right thing" only to end up feeling wrong?

I didn't know it yet, but I was about to go even deeper into the fire.

Part III: When Journals Cry

"This is what it sounds like... when doves cry."

— Prince, Purple Rain (1984)

Not long after this phase, I reconnected with my **first wife.**

She and I had kept in loose contact after going no contact for 6 years.

I met my second wife through my first wife.

Let that sink in.

My first wife loved herself some reggae music. Loved it to a fault, really. She had her favorite bands, knew the setlists by heart, followed the scene like it was part of her spiritual practice. One of her favorite groups played locally often, and she started noticing the same young woman showing up to all the shows. Stylish. Energetic. Always near the front. Eventually, they became friendly—concert buddies bonded by rhythm and good vibes.

My first wife always mentioned the rock on that girl's hand. "She was definitely engaged," she'd say. "That ring? Huge. No question." So in her mind, this woman wasn't a factor—spoken for, unavailable, harmless. When the chance came up, she introduced us, thinking nothing of it.

She had no idea what she was setting in motion.

I saw something in this woman. Something magnetic. When I asked about her, that's when my first wife learned that the engagement had ended and the woman was very much single.

We started talking. It clicked. She was a veteran too. She understood the structure, the pace, the unspoken sacrifices. There was a comfort there—like she got me before I even explained myself. We dated for three months.

And then we got married.

This time, I wanted to do it right. No shortcuts. No pride. No assumptions. I didn't want to repeat my past, so I tried to do better. One of my good friends gave me some simple advice: "Start journaling."

So I did.

I wrote about everything—the good, the cracks, the patterns I didn't want to admit I recognized. I wrote when we argued. I wrote about her sharp edges. I wrote about the ways I was folding myself just to keep things smooth. The journal became the only safe place I had to speak my truth, even when I couldn't face it aloud.

At the same time, I leaned hard into the spiritual side of things. We did premarital counseling. I brought in pastors. I listened to advisors. I gave God control—or so I thought. Every time something felt off, I chalked it up to fear, not truth. I drowned red flags in prayer.

I thought I was being faithful.

I thought I was erring on the side of obedience.

But I was abandoning myself again.

Six months into the marriage, she became pregnant.

I was shocked—but happy. I felt like this was the sign that we were on the right path. A course correction. A blessing. A reason to believe again.

She didn't see it that way.

She didn't want to keep the baby.

There was no discussion. No mutual decision-making. No kneeling together in prayer. Just her choice. And once she made it, there was no undoing it.

She got the abortion—against my will.

And I stood by her. I supported her. I drove her. I told myself I was being a good husband, a godly man. But inside, I was unraveling.

Then came the whispers.

Some of my closest friends pulled me aside, gently, cautiously.

"Bruh… you sure it was yours?"

"I'm just saying… the math ain't mathing."

"Why'd she rush it like that?"

I shut it down. I refused to question it. If she was my wife, then it was my child. Period. I wasn't built to entertain betrayal like that. But deep down, something was shifting. Something dark. Something cold.

I was **shattered.**

She had always been the "spiritual one."

The one who led.

The one who preached.

And here she was, doing something that violated the very principles she claimed to live by.

I wasn't just angry at her.

I was **furious with God.**

I had followed God. I had followed counsel. I had done "everything right."

And I got burned anyway.

So I made a decision.

I didn't rage. I didn't throw anything. I didn't even argue. I just started planning her exit. Quietly. Strategically. Shortly after the "INCIDENT", I got assigned to a new duty station and told her I needed time to settle in. I told her I would get counseling (because I clearly was the problem) and that I'd send for her.

But I had no intention of doing that.

As soon as I landed at my new post, I filed for divorce.

But I couldn't finalize it right away—state law required six months of residency before I could proceed. Not two months into my new assignment I got temporary relocation orders for a six-month deployment to Bosnia. I left, assuming everything would sit still.

But my attorney didn't forget.

Six months later, I was divorced. Just like that.

She never saw it coming.

Word got back to me downrange, that she showed up at my duty station later—furious, blindsided, demanding answers. But by then, the system had already caught up. She was no longer listed as my dependent. No longer entitled to base access or benefits. No longer anything.

And I didn't feel guilt.

I didn't feel relief either.

I just felt... nothing.

I had gone numb.

Somewhere along the way, I stopped believing that God was protecting me. I stopped believing that faith worked. I stopped trusting anything outside my own plans.

Between 1999 and 2007—the years I call the "**Lost Years**"—I had no spirituality.

No connection.

No prayer.

No compass.

I shut down emotionally.

Shut down spiritually.

I didn't even pretend to be "working on myself."

And then, I found it.

The journal.

The one I started when I met her.

The same journal I kept when I met my second wife.

The one I thought I lost.

I flipped through the pages—and it wrecked me.

Because I saw it all:

The warnings. The flags. The gut feelings.

I had written, in my own handwriting, exactly what I felt—what I feared.

And then I saw where I ignored it all in the name of God.

I broke my own rules.

I silenced my own wisdom.

I chose blindness.

And called it "faith."

When I opened it, I didn't just read it—I remembered. The doubts. The gut feelings. The red flags I silenced in the name of love, faith, and community. It was all there. In ink. In my own handwriting.

And that's when the real heartbreak set in.

Because I didn't fail because I was deceived.

I failed because I knew—and I ignored it anyway.

In the name of obedience.

In the name of spiritual order.

In the name of love.

I overrode my gut.

I abandoned my voice.

And God didn't stop me.

That's when I stopped praying.

Stopped listening.

Stopped believing.

Because I didn't trust anyone anymore.

Not her.

Not the church.

Not even God. Especially NOT God!

Only the journal had been honest.

That journal became my personal ghost.

I told every woman I dated after that that I was **emotionally unavailable.**

I meant it.

I was prepared to **retire in 2007** after 20 years in the military and disappear from the world.

My plan?

Move to **Australia.**

Sail yachts for a buddy in the Whitsundays.

No relationships. No drama.

Just saltwater and freedom.

But as life would have it… that's not how the story ends.

Chapter 6

The House We Didn't Build

Part I: A Wedding, A Wound, and A World Apart

I wasn't looking to get married again. But I wasn't closed to it either. At that stage in my life, I had one goal: get through the last stretch of military service and disappear. I had mapped out my freedom in vivid detail—sell everything, move to Australia, and spend my days sailing boats up and down the Whitsundays to Sydney. No more war zones. No more bureaucracy. No more trying to save people who didn't want to be saved.

I wasn't jaded—I was just done.

So when I met her, I wasn't searching for a partner. But I also didn't resist the connection when it came. It didn't feel like fate. It didn't feel smooth. It felt... real. Messy. Tangled. Human.

We didn't always get along. In fact, we clashed often. But there was something about her—something grounded, something enduring. I couldn't name it then. I just knew I didn't want to lose it.

We got married in 2008. Twice.

Once in May, at the Alameda County Courthouse in Oakland. That was practical—a military move to secure her benefits. No flowers. No ceremony. Just paperwork and purpose.

Then again in August, this time in Cancun. Family, sun, sand, and a ceremony that felt like it belonged in a photo album. We made promises in front of everyone, dressed in beige and white, with ocean wind in our faces. It felt hopeful. Maybe even redemptive.

But our story didn't wait long to unravel.

On July 7, 2009—just two days after her birthday—everything changed.

We were in San Francisco for her cousin's baby shower, enjoying what was supposed to be a lighthearted vacation. But that morning, she went into congestive heart failure. One minute we were celebrating new life, the next we were facing a life-or-death emergency.

Because of her condition, she was medically prohibited from flying. She couldn't return to Washington, D.C., where we had been living. Instead, she went north—to Seattle—so she could be cared for by her parents.

That was the day our lives split. No warning. No choice. From that point forward, we began living apart.

Once again, I found myself asking, "God… why her? Why now? Why me again?"

After everything I had survived—war, divorce, betrayal—I thought I'd earned some peace. I thought this marriage was supposed to be my do-over. Instead, I was back in survival mode. Only this time, I wasn't the one sick—but I was the one drowning.

We lived apart for the next few years. From July 2009 to 2011.

Years of strained phone calls, time-zone gaps, and emotional gaps even wider.

Part II: The In-Laws and the Invisible

By 2011, I was finally able to relocate to **Seattle** and be with my wife again.

But instead of us building a home together, I moved into hers.

More accurately, her *parents'* home.

She lived in the basement.

I joined her there.

Let me be clear—I understood the logic.

She had just come through a life-threatening crisis.

Being close to her parents made sense medically, emotionally, logistically.

But for me?

It was suffocating.

I felt like I was living in someone else's shadow.

Like a guest in my own marriage.

Like a child playing house in someone else's home.

My wife was being cared for.

I was being watched.

Everything I did felt monitored—judged.

It didn't matter that I was a grown man with a career, a military pension, and decades of service.

Under their roof, I was just the husband in the basement.

I suggested moving.

No one agreed.

Not her. Not her parents.

Not the doctors.

So I did what I'd been trained to do in the military:

I put the mission before the man.

The needs of the group over the needs of the self.

I stayed.

I shut down.

I disappeared into myself again.

That's when the financial fracture happened.

A misunderstanding between her, me, and her parents—at least, that's what it was called. But to me, it felt like betrayal. Promises were made. Boundaries were crossed. And suddenly, the family I had folded myself into felt like strangers holding my future in their hands.

It confirmed what I feared most:

I didn't belong.

I wasn't trusted.

And I wasn't in control.

That basement became both a refuge and a crucible.

It protected her.

It suffocated me.

Living under their roof came with rules—spoken and unspoken. I wasn't the man of the house. I wasn't even sure I felt like a man in that house. My wife was being nurtured back to health by the people who raised her—and I was just a respectful visitor passing through.

I tried to make it work.

Tried to be grateful.

Tried to suppress the resentment building inside me.

But it grew.

I didn't feel seen. I didn't feel respected. And even when I said as much, it felt like I was being told to suck it up. That her healing mattered more than my discomfort.

Part III: Broken Promises and Spiritual Drifting

I tried to hold on.

Tried to be patient.

Tried to believe that this was just another trial—that God would show up and deliver us into a healthier season.

But every time I extended grace, I felt violated.

Every time I gave the benefit of the doubt, I got burned.

And I couldn't ignore the deeper question gnawing at me:

Why was I led here?

Why was I drawn to this woman—only to be wounded again?

Why had I sacrificed my plans, my peace, my presence of mind… just to feel like a stranger in my own life?

Once again, I blamed **God.**

I had asked for signs.

I had tried to do the right thing.

I stayed when I should have left.

I submitted when I should have stood up.

I prioritized the relationship when I should have protected myself.

And for what?

At the lowest point, I couldn't even pray.

I didn't want guidance.

I wanted *justice*.

I withdrew emotionally. I became colder. Not out of malice—but because I had no more margin for heartbreak.

But somewhere between the resentment and the silence, life crept back in.

And still… we stayed together.

Through the miscommunication.

Through the illness.

Through the distance and the disillusionment.

And slowly—miraculously—something else started to take root.

We had a son.

We survived her heart transplant.

We made it through COVID.

Not perfectly. Not without scars. But together.

I won't pretend I found God again in those moments. There was no blinding light, no holy revelation. Just… moments.

Moments that whispered to me instead of shouting.

Like watching my son sleep and realizing I was needed.

Like holding her hand in the ICU and realizing I wasn't ready to lose her.

Like praying—not because I was desperate, but because I wanted to believe again.

It wasn't a spiritual rebirth.

It was a reconstruction.

Not rebuilding what was broken, but building something honest.

Something with scars and boundaries and truth.

And for once—I wasn't asking anyone else how to do it.

This time, I was using my own blueprints.

Because for the first time in a long time…

I wasn't just angry at God.

I was listening again.

Chapter 7

Yes-Yallin' and the Therapist Who Called It Out

Before classes even started at UCLA, I made a decision that would change everything: **I got a therapist**. But not just any therapist—I had requirements.

They had to:

- Understand the **military**.
- Be **African American**.
- Have graduated from an **HBCU**.

That might sound like a tall order to some, but the universe delivered.

She matched all three.

And she was local.

From our first conversation, I knew she saw through me.

Not in a threatening way, but in a "don't even try to front" kind of way.

I didn't have to translate my military speech.

Didn't have to explain what it means to feel like a cultural outlier.

Didn't have to justify my anger, or my grief, or why I operated the way I did.

She just… got it.

And that made all the difference.

One of the first things we dug into was my people-pleasing.

Not the kind that says, "Sure, I'll help you move a couch."

No, this was **soul-deep pleasing**.

I said yes when I meant no.

I agreed when I wanted to disappear.

I showed up when I was empty.

I made my peace the price for their comfort.

And one day, after I had recounted yet another situation where I overextended myself and felt drained afterward, my therapist asked me:

"Dennis… when was the last time you said no… without guilt?"

I couldn't answer.

Not because I didn't know.

But because I had **never done it.**

Ever.

She said, "Don't rush. Think on it. Tell me next week."

Next week came.

Still no answer.

That silence told her everything.

And it told me everything too.

Somewhere between childhood and command posts, I had internalized the idea that my value came from **doing.**

And doing well.

And doing quietly.

And doing without complaint.

You were strong.

You were sharp.

You were dependable.

And if you were *really good* at being dependable?

People just assumed you'd carry more. No questions asked.

That's what I did.

And I did it for decades.

Military. Government. Marriage. Community work. Friends. Family.

And all that "yes-ing"?

That was "yes-yallin."

Straight out of the 80s hip-hop era.

The "Yes yes y'all… and you don't stop…" type of pleasing.

Except I didn't stop.

I kept yes-yallin' myself right into emotional bankruptcy.

At the same time this inner work was unfolding, I had just been accepted into a global graduate program.

And as part of that, we had an **international travel component.**

I walked into that classroom already cracked open.

What happened next? That's when the flood came.

It started innocently enough. One of my classmates asked if I wanted to travel together before our international course began. It sounded fun. Light. Easy.

And after all, I was trying to do things differently…for education's sake.

Say yes more because its all about networking.

Open up more.

Trust more.

So I did.

And that's when things got complicated.

It wasn't just a trip.

It was a pressure cooker.

There was drama. There were arguments. And while I wasn't the source of it, I often became the "safe" place to vent, the one asked to mediate, to offer perspective, to "be the adult in the room."

I didn't sign up for that.

My role was supposed to be light—be a travel companion, a sounding board maybe, help someone navigate their group dynamics without becoming part of them.

But that line blurred quickly.

One moment I was a trusted confidant. The next, I was pulled into conflicts that had nothing to do with me—except I was now expected to manage their emotional weight.

Here was someone who said all the right things—spiritual this, inner peace that, healing journeys and trauma-informed that. But their actions rarely matched their words.

At first, I brushed it off. I told myself not to be judgmental. That I was projecting.

But the discomfort grew.

Subtle dismissals. Hot-and-cold behavior. Cycles of closeness followed by stone walls.

And through it all, I kept trying to be the stabilizer.

Kept trying to help.

Kept ignoring the knot in my chest.

I didn't know it then, but those were red flags.

Now, I know better.

The problem wasn't just the red flags. It was that I didn't have boundaries. I never learned what they were. I'd grown up in systems where obedience was praised and personal needs were buried. Whether it was church, the military, or marriage—I was taught to adapt, endure, and serve.

I thought that made me strong.

But in those hotel rooms, halfway across the world, I realized it had also made me vulnerable.

I was trying to earn love by being safe. By being the protector. By being the one who stayed calm, stayed steady, stayed available—even when I was hurting.

And in the end? I was left shattered.

Not because they broke me.

But because I had no idea how to protect myself.

But therapy didn't just help me process what happened. It helped me recognize what I'd been doing all my life.

When I came back home and unpacked the trip with my therapist, she didn't say "I told you so."

She didn't criticize me for trusting too fast.

She said:

"You didn't know how to set boundaries—because no one ever taught you that you were allowed to."

And that hit me hard.

In the **military,** your people have your back.

You don't need to build a wall around yourself.

You are the wall—for each other.

But in the real world?

People don't play by those rules.

And I had never learned how to **protect myself** from people who didn't live by honor, by loyalty, or by code.

I thought "watching your six" was universal.

It wasn't.

The lesson?

Boundaries aren't selfish.

They're sacred.

And if you don't build them,

you'll keep yes-yallin' yourself into relationships, careers, and emotional contracts that were never meant to serve you.

But the question came up again…

"Dennis… when was the last time you said no—without guilt?"

The great thing about therapists—good ones—is that over time, they really get to know all the details of what's going on in your life. They remember things you forgot you mentioned. They track your patterns even when you're still busy justifying them.

So when she asked me that question, she wasn't just making small talk.

She was holding up a truth I'd never dared to see.

I tried to laugh it off. I reached for an example. Nothing came.

She didn't push. She just said:

"Don't rush the answer. Tell me next week."

A week later, I got back on the Zoom…

She asked again.

"Did you come up with a time?"

I shook my head.

"Still nothing," I said.

"And I guess… that's the point."

That silence between us said more than any list of examples ever could. I wasn't just uncomfortable saying no—I didn't even know how. Saying yes had become my identity. Saying yes made me useful. Saying yes kept me needed, safe, accepted.

That 'yes-yallin'' wasn't just habit.

It was a performance. A rhythm I learned somewhere between Sunday school and boom boxes.

A way to make myself palatable to people who didn't always see me.

And over time, it stopped sounding like me at all.

All that yes-yallin'—

Trying to keep peace, keep face, keep from being replaced—

Was costing me pieces of myself I didn't even know I had given away.

In the weeks that followed, my therapy sessions got heavier. My dreams got more vivid. My memories came rushing back—moments I hadn't thought about in decades.

But for the first time, I didn't run.

I didn't numb.

I stayed with the pain.

Because now, I could name it.

And once you can name something, you can heal it.

The mirror wasn't my classmate.

It wasn't the classroom.

It wasn't even the heartbreak.

The mirror was me—

Stripped of my titles, my training, and my trauma armor.

And what I saw…

Wasn't weakness.

It was the beginning of freedom.

Chapter 8

Power Plays and Passovers

Obedience used to be my superpower. I was good at it. Real good. It started in childhood—when silence was praised and questioning was punished. In the military, that same obedience was promoted into rank. In marriage, it was repackaged as selflessness. In church, it was called faith.

Follow the rules.

Don't rock the boat.

Don't ask too many questions.

Don't make people uncomfortable.

Obedience got me medals, promotions, titles, access.

It got me respect.

But it also got me stuck.

Because here's the part they never teach you:

Obedience without reflection becomes bondage.

And I had no idea how deeply bound I was.

Looking back, I can see how obedience shaped everything—from how I handled betrayal, to how I gave away my voice in relationships, to how I stayed in jobs, roles, and environments long past their expiration date.

Even my spiritual life was soaked in it.

I didn't explore God—I executed Him like a checklist.

Church? Check.

Pray? Check.

Tithe? Check.

Conflicted? Quietly suffer.

The weight of obedience isn't just heavy. It's invisible.

You carry it without realizing how it bends your posture, compresses your breath, shrinks your capacity to dream.

But when I started therapy, and even more so in grad school, that weight started showing up in ways I couldn't ignore anymore.

Like how I felt guilty saying no.

Like how I volunteered for things I didn't want to do.

Like how I shrank when I should've spoken up.

Like how I kept thinking my suffering was noble—as if suffering was proof of love, or faith, or strength.

And the worst part?

I wasn't doing it out of fear.

I was doing it out of conditioning.

I believed that obedience made me worthy.

But obedience without discernment is not loyalty—it's erasure.

It's self-abandonment dressed up as sacrifice.

And when I finally saw that?

I had to grieve.

I had to get angry.

I had to start unlearning.

Because the real me—the intuitive, discerning, boundary-drawing, question-asking me—was buried under decades of "Yes, sir," "Amen," and "Whatever you need."

This chapter of my life wasn't about rebellion.

It wasn't about flipping tables or burning bridges.

It was about one small, powerful shift:

Choosing alignment over approval.

I didn't have to reject structure to reclaim myself.

I just had to stop disappearing inside it.

I used to think integrity and obedience walked hand in hand.

But over time, I started to see they didn't always lead to the same destination.

Like the time I was up for promotion to Lieutenant Colonel.

The chatter started early—how to get ahead, how to "game" the system in a way that still looked clean on paper. Officers were whispering about a loophole—if you could get reassigned to a senior rater with an "immature profile," someone who hadn't rated many others yet, your chances of getting a "top block" increased. No competition. No record to compare against. A guaranteed boost.

All it took was 90 days.

Technically, it was allowable.

There's a certain unspoken game that happens when you're up for promotion in the military—especially once you hit that O-4 to O-5 zone.

Everybody knows the rules.

Everybody pretends they don't.

But trust me, they're there.

I was up for promotion to **Lieutenant Colonel (LTC).**

And while I had done the work, carried the weight, and built a career I was proud of, I started noticing a pattern.

Other officers—ones just like me, some even junior—were suddenly getting **"top block"** evaluations.

Not from their original senior raters, mind you.

From new ones.

On paper, it all looked clean.

A 90-day assignment. A shift in command.

But what was really happening?

They were **gaming the system.**

Here's how it worked:

If you could get reassigned to a senior rater who had a **clean profile**—meaning, they hadn't rated many people yet—you had a shot at being their "top block" without competing against a stacked record.

It was **legal.**

But it wasn't **honorable.**

And I knew it.

People approached me about it.

Told me, "You should look for a clean profile. You've earned this."

But something in me—*the old soldier, the believer in merit, the part of me still clinging to a moral code*—said no.

I couldn't do it.

I had spent too many years preaching about leadership, about doing things the right way, about not cutting corners just because you can.

And now I was being asked to cut a corner…

for myself.

Ethically, I couldn't stomach it.

That's not how I was raised. That's not how I served.

I didn't join the military to climb through backdoors.

I didn't survive deployments to cheat on paper.

So I stayed where I was.

Took the honest path.

Let the system speak for itself.

So I declined.

I stayed with my rater.

I didn't play the game.

And guess what?

I didn't get promoted.

It stung. Not just because I was passed over—but because I knew deep down, I'd made the "right" choice… and it didn't matter.

That's when the weight of obedience really hit me.

I wasn't just obeying orders—I was obeying a principle I'd been taught to revere.

And that obedience cost me something measurable. Tangible. Professional.

It made me question everything:

Was I loyal… or just naïve?

Was I principled… or just playing a losing game?

And yet, if I had to do it over again, I still wouldn't chase the workaround.

Because obedience, for me, had always been tied to honor.

Even when that honor didn't pay off.

But man… carrying that weight?

Knowing you were passed over because you chose integrity?

That's a heavy truth no one prepares you for.

I didn't show it at the time—military bearing and all—but I was crushed.

Not because I felt I needed the rank to validate my service.

But because I saw others who didn't hold the same values **win.**

I saw people I wouldn't trust with a platoon get the "top block."

I saw the system reward maneuvering more than merit.

It wasn't just a career disappointment.

It was a **spiritual gut-check.**

I went home.

I sat in the silence.

And I asked the same question I always asked when things didn't add up:

"God… why?"

Why let me do everything right—

only to watch others succeed by doing it wrong?

Why give me conviction—

if it was just going to hold me back?

Why ask for obedience—

and then pass me over?

What I didn't realize at the time was that this wasn't about the **rank**.

It was about the **refinement**.

The military had been the first system I gave my life to.

But it wouldn't be the last.

And if I was going to survive what came after—corporate systems, nonprofit boards, relationships, betrayals—I needed to understand this one truth:

Doing the right thing does not guarantee a reward.

But doing the wrong thing guarantees a cost.

And for me?

My peace of mind was worth more than an O-5 pin.

Looking back, I see now that being passed over didn't diminish me.

It protected me—from losing myself in a system that was never built to honor who I truly was.

I didn't get promoted.

But I didn't sell my soul either.

And in this phase of my life, that's the kind of promotion that actually matters.

Chapter 9

The Return to Self

It's funny what your body knows—long before your mind catches up. For years, I'd been telling myself I was fine. Functional. Resilient. Tough.

But I was living in a constant state of low-grade burnout.

I wasn't joyful.

I wasn't peaceful.

I was just **managing.**

And then, one day, I stopped managing.

Not with a meltdown.

Not with a declaration.

But with a whisper of surrender.

I had a case of the **"fuck-its."**

That phrase—"the fuck-its"—goes back to my days as a young lieutenant.

Me and one of my closest Army buddies used to say it when everything around us was so absurd, so overloaded, or so far out of our control that the only rational response was to emotionally *check out.*

"Man, I got a case of the fuck-its," we'd say with a crooked smile.

It was our pressure valve.

Our way of admitting that we were at the **end of our care rope.**

That nothing we did would change the outcome—so why keep fighting?

Back then, it was about bureaucracy.

About impossible logistics.

About dumb decisions coming from the top.

But now?

The "fuck-its" weren't about the Army.

They were about **me.**

I wasn't just tired of bad decisions.

I was tired of **abandoning myself.**

I realized that I'd spent a lifetime making calculated choices to survive, to succeed, to be seen as someone who always had it together.

But when I finally started *really* doing the work—therapy, reflection, journaling—I realized something devastating:

I had trusted my instincts in every domain except when it came to **me.**

In combat? My gut kept me alive.

With money? My gut protected my future.

On the job? My gut told me who to avoid and when to speak up.

But when it came to **my own emotional needs,** my own boundaries, my own energy?

I ignored the voice every time.

And the more I ignored it, the more my inner world shrank.

Until I was living not from passion… but from **pattern.**

That pattern looked like this:
- Be useful.
- Be strong.
- Be silent.
- Be agreeable.
- Don't rock the boat.
- Don't say no.
- Don't need too much.
- Don't show pain.

And underneath all that?

A man who was tired of saving everyone else… while no one saved him.

The return to self wasn't a big moment.

It didn't come with fireworks or some dramatic awakening.

It came quietly.

Like one morning when I woke up and realized I didn't want to prove anything to anyone that day.

Or when I said "no" to a request without explaining myself—and noticed I didn't feel guilty.

Or when I stopped asking if people would still like me… and started asking if **I liked them.**

Little things.

But each one was a brick in a house I was finally building for **me.**

That's what Chapter 9 represents.

Not a fall.

Not a comeback.

But a **homecoming.**

Not to the soldier.

Not to the husband.

Not to the community leader.

But to Dennis.

The one behind all the armor.

The one who was still standing—quietly, patiently—waiting to be remembered.

Chapter 10

Learning to Love Without Losing Yourself

There's a certain kind of freedom that doesn't come from escaping others—it comes from finally **returning to yourself.** After all the heartbreak, all the betrayals, all the over-giving and under-receiving relationships, I had one pressing question left:

Can I love people… without abandoning myself?

That's where this chapter begins.

When you've spent most of your life in uniforms—literal or symbolic—stripping them off doesn't always feel like freedom. Sometimes it feels like getting naked in front of a mirror you've avoided for years.

That's what this part of the journey felt like.

I wasn't just questioning my beliefs anymore.

I was questioning me.

Not the version of me who knew how to "yes-sir" through chaos.

Not the polished version who gave speeches and wrote proposals and kept his pain tucked in at the corners.

But the me who had been hiding beneath layers of survival for decades.

And what I found?

I barely knew him.

For so long, my identity had been shaped by systems—military, marriage, ministry, mission. And I played every part to the best of my ability. I got medals. I got degrees. I got promotions. I got praise.

But I didn't get peace.

Because I was still waiting for someone else to validate me.

Still waiting for the next checkpoint to tell me I was on track.

Still waiting for permission to rest. To breathe. To be.

And the wildest part?

I was the one holding the keys all along.

Therapy cracked it open. Heartbreak made it bleed. But it was the quiet moments—those still, almost forgettable moments—that started bringing me back to myself.

Moments like:
- Laughing with my son without checking the time.
- Writing without wondering who would approve.
- Saying "no" and not explaining why.

- Walking outside and not having to carry any title but "man."

In the past, my pattern was simple:
- Meet someone.
- Feel needed.
- Overextend.
- Lose myself.
- Crash.

- Repeat.

I didn't know what boundaries were—not really.

I thought boundaries were walls.

Or ultimatums.

Or things you put up when you didn't trust people.

This was the me I'd abandoned.

Not out of malice—but out of necessity.

Because survival doesn't leave room for self-discovery.

And yet, here he was—waiting. Still intact. Still worthy. Still mine.

This return to self wasn't loud or dramatic.

There was no movie montage or spiritual thunderclap.

It was a slow homecoming.

A quiet reunion.

A rebuilding from the inside out.

And the most surprising part?

I didn't have to go on a pilgrimage or meditate on a mountain.

I just had to say yes to the things that lit me up—even if they made no sense to anyone else.

Like the time I took an intermediate tap dance class.

No reason. No explanation. I just felt like it.

There I was, feet clacking across the floor with a room full of strangers, no goal in mind but rhythm. For that hour, I wasn't a veteran, a father, a husband, or a student. I was just a man listening to the beat of his own shoes.

No reason.

No backstory.

Just something I wanted to do.

And the next weekend?

An **improvisation class.**

Me.

In a room with strangers.

No script.

No prep.

Just presence.

I laughed.

I danced.

I forgot how heavy the world was.

And for once—I didn't need to **explain** it.

Didn't need it to be part of some plan.

Didn't need to justify the time spent or the joy it gave.

I was simply living.

These classes weren't just hobbies.

They were **healing in motion.**

Each shuffle of my tap shoes…

Each unscripted line in an improv circle…

Was a way to reclaim the parts of me I'd long buried beneath other people's expectations.

For so long, I thought love was **sacrifice.**

But now I know real love includes **selfhood.**

If I can't be me—fully, unapologetically, joyfully—then it's not love.

It's performance.

And I've done enough performing for a lifetime.

I still want love.

I still want partnership.

But I no longer want it at the cost of my peace.

I want someone to join me on the road I've paved with truth, therapy, tenderness, and time.

Not someone who wants to drive me back into silence.

So yes…

I'm learning to love again.

But this time, I'm loving with boundaries.

With presence.

With discernment.

With grace.

And most importantly—

Without losing myself.

I started asking new questions:

- What do I enjoy—without obligation?

- What feels right in my body—not just my mind?

- Who do I trust to see me, not just need me?

The answers weren't always clear.

But they were mine.

And that was new.

This part of the journey wasn't about becoming someone else.

It was about remembering who I was before the world taught me to forget.

But what I've learned is this:

Boundaries aren't about others.

They're about self-respect.

And it was time I learned to love from a place of **wholeness**, not habit.

Chapter 11

Loving Without Losing: Choosing Peace

I used to think love was about sacrifice. That's what I was taught—at church, in the military, in my family. You give. You serve. You protect. You show up even when it costs you.

And sometimes?

You disappear—bit by bit—because you think that's what devotion looks like.

That was my blueprint for love.

It was noble. It was honorable.

And it almost destroyed me.

Because no one ever told me that love without boundaries isn't love.

It's erosion.

And I was the one washing away.

Every relationship—romantic, familial, even professional—I showed up ready to give everything. My time. My energy. My wisdom. My loyalty. My heart. I gave so much that when I was betrayed or abandoned, it wasn't just loss I felt—it was vacancy. Like someone had walked off with pieces of me I hadn't realized I'd handed over.

And the wildest part?

I didn't even know how to stop doing it.

Until recently.

Until I started telling the truth about the cost of that kind of love.

Until I started noticing the patterns.

How often I ignored my gut.

How often I tried to fix instead of feel.

How often I said "yes" when my spirit was screaming "don't."

I started asking myself different questions:
- Can I love someone and still say no?
- Can I be generous without being depleted?
- Can I stay if staying means silencing myself?

But here's what shook me…

I had always trusted my instincts—on the battlefield, in high-stakes situations, even in money matters.

My gut had saved lives.

My decisions had earned promotions.

But when it came to me?

My emotional safety?

My heart?

My peace?

I abandoned my instincts like they didn't belong to me.

Because I was never taught to protect myself emotionally.

In the military, you didn't have to.

You had your unit. Your battle buddy. Your team.

Someone always had your six.

The assumption was built in—they've got me.

So I never developed the internal reflex to question whether I was safe. I assumed I was.

And for a long time, I brought that same trust into my relationships.

But the truth is…

Most people don't operate by those rules.

They weren't trained to stand guard for someone else.

They weren't taught to die on the hill for the group.

They weren't issued the same code.

So while I was showing up like a soldier—loyal, protective, all-in—

I was often surrounded by people playing by civilian rules.

Every man for himself. Every woman for herself. Survival of the individual.

And I kept getting wounded, not because love is a battlefield—

But because I was treating it like a basecamp.

I expected people to defend me the way I defended them.

And when they didn't?

I took it as a failure of me, not a mismatch in values.

It never dawned on me that I needed protection around myself—

Just like we built berms and defensive positions around every forward operating base.

I was the only unsecured perimeter in my own life.

Now, I know:

Love is not supposed to feel like debt.

Love is not a hunger that only you are supposed to feed.

Love is not a performance with pain as the price of entry.

Love is a mirror.

Love is a boundary.

Love is being able to say, "I still matter, even here."

So these days, I'm practicing something new.

I don't chase.

I don't beg.

I don't barter my peace for attention.

I show up full—and expect to be met.

I love out loud—but I don't silence my own voice to make someone else feel more comfortable.

I open my heart—but not at the cost of closing my spirit.

And if someone can't handle the real me?

I don't shrink.

I don't explain.

I don't contort.

I let them go.

Because love that requires my disappearance… isn't love at all.

Chapter 12

Rewriting the Rules

At some point, I realized I was still living by rules I never agreed to. Rules I inherited. Rules I absorbed. Rules that were handed to me by the church, the Army, my family, the world. They were written in invisible ink—unspoken, but enforced.

- Be strong, even when you're breaking.
- Be obedient, even when it doesn't make sense.
- Be dependable, even when you're depleted.
- Be a man, even if it means being numb.

And I followed them. For decades.

Because I thought that's what made me good.

What made me useful. What made me safe.

But those rules didn't protect me.

They confined me.

They taught me how to perform—but not how to feel.

How to serve—but not how to receive.

How to hold everyone else—but not how to hold myself.

And when those rules stopped working?

When they cost me peace, clarity, joy?

I didn't just feel betrayed—I felt lost.

Because I didn't know what else to live by.

That's when I had to sit down—like really sit down—and ask:

If the old rules no longer serve me…

What does?

What if masculinity isn't about toughness, but tenderness with edges?

What if leadership isn't about control, but clarity?

What if faith isn't about obedience, but relationship?

What if love isn't earned… but received freely, with discernment?

So I started rewriting the rules.

One by one. Quietly. Internally.

Not for the world—but for me.

New rules like:
- If my body tightens, my spirit is speaking.
- Silence is not always strength—sometimes it's suppression.
- I am allowed to change my mind.
- I do not have to explain my "no."
- Peace is not a reward—it's a requirement.
- Being needed is not the same as being valued.
- I don't owe anyone access to the parts of me they've proven they can't honor.

Some of these rules were hard to adopt.

They challenged everything I'd been praised for.

They made me feel selfish, defiant, even disloyal.

But they also made me feel free.

Evidence of a Shift

But these weren't just mental shifts.

Looking back now, I see the changes didn't start in my head.

They started in my spirit—almost silently.

Like something deep inside me was making choices I hadn't caught up to yet.

I remember walking through a local Black business market one weekend and stopping at a vendor's table. Handmade jewelry. Soul chains, they called them. I wasn't there looking for anything in particular, but I walked away with two.

One was a crown chakra crystal—meant to cleanse and clear the upper realms of consciousness.

The other? Black tourmaline—used to protect and ground the root chakra.

I bought them without hesitation. And they weren't cheap.

What struck me later wasn't the purchase.

It was the why.

I didn't grow up buying healing crystals. I wasn't raised to believe in chakras, energy fields, or soul alignment. And yet... something in me moved toward them. Trusted them. Knew them.

It made me wonder:

Was something trapped inside me trying to come out?

Something spiritual I hadn't yet given language to?

Was this part of me always there… just waiting for permission?

The signs kept coming.

I found myself listening to affirmations before bed.

I started watching Sadguru, then Bashar, then other voices I'd once have dismissed.

I explored tarot.

I stretched into yoga poses, even though my body resisted.

I tried meditation, not to be still—but to listen for something I couldn't hear in the noise.

None of it was part of the script I was raised on.

But every piece of it felt like remembering.

Like my soul was finally stretching after a long sleep.

These weren't trends.

They were markers.

Proof that I was changing.

Not in a flash.

But in a series of quiet choices that said:

"I'm ready for more."

And then something else started happening.

I stopped just asking for things from the universe…

and started acting like they were already mine.

I'd imagine the future I wanted—and then I'd start walking like it was already here.

I'd dress like it.

Speak like it.

Make decisions as if the vision had already arrived.

It wasn't arrogance.

It was alignment.

A shift from hoping… to embodying.

I wasn't waiting to be seen as worthy, powerful, abundant, or whole.

I started moving as if I already was.

And I'll be honest: I haven't perfected that. Not even close.

But when I do lean into it—when I show up like I'm already the man I'm becoming?

Things move.

People appear.

Doors creak open.

Call it energy. Call it faith. Call it alignment.

All I know is…

It's real.

And it's mine now.

And the wildest part?

It's not just that new things are showing up.

It's that old things are quietly slipping away.

People. Habits. Beliefs.

Some just… disappear.

Not because I banished them.

Not because I slammed the door.

But because I stopped orbiting in their direction.

They fall away like expired weight.

Like roles I no longer audition for.

Like noise I no longer hear.

And I've learned not to chase what leaves.

Not everything is meant to make it to the next chapter.

Sometimes, freedom is not about what you go get—

It's about what finally lets go of you.

Chapter 13

Redemption Is a Quiet Thing

I used to think redemption had to be dramatic. That it had to look like some big, sweeping moment— falling on your knees in church, weeping through an apology,

getting it all "right" after years of getting it wrong.

That's how I was taught to recognize redemption.

Loud. Painful. Public.

But that's not how it came to me.

Redemption showed up quietly.

It showed up on a Tuesday afternoon when I didn't spiral.

It showed up when I said "no" and didn't explain myself.

It showed up when I looked in the mirror and didn't flinch.

Redemption wasn't a grand return.

It was a soft release.

Of guilt.

Of performance.

Of needing to prove I was worth saving.

It came the moment I stopped trying to "earn" grace

and started living like it was already mine.

For a long time, I thought I had to fix everything in order to be whole.

That my story had to wrap up in a clean arc.

That I had to have the answers.

But what I've learned is that wholeness isn't perfection.

It's permission.

Permission to carry both the wounds and the wisdom.

To be flawed and faithful.

To hold grief in one hand and hope in the other.

To love again, even when you remember what it cost the last time.

Redemption came when I stopped hiding.

Not from the world—but from myself.

When I could finally say:
- Yes, I failed at some things.
- Yes, I hurt and was hurt.
- Yes, I've been the villain and the victim.
- Yes, I've healed… and yes, I still have work to do.

But I'm not ashamed of the road anymore.

Because I know now—this story matters.

Not just the polished parts.

The whole story.

Even the mess.

Especially the mess.

And if redemption doesn't come crashing in… sometimes, you write it yourself.

Literally.

I've written letters to people I hurt and never saw again.

One to a girl in my 7th grade English class—someone I insulted without knowing how deeply I wounded her.

She left the school not long after, and while no one ever blamed me out loud…

I knew.

My words crushed her spirit. And I've carried that.

So I wrote her a letter.

Apologizing. Owning it. Releasing it.

It wasn't for performance.

It was for peace.

And that wasn't the only letter.

I wrote one to a UCLA classmate—the one who cracked open my shadow self.

I thanked them.

For revealing the places I had abandoned myself.

For being the mirror that showed how much I bent, gave, and broke just to be liked.

How I wore people-pleasing like a badge of honor, and how much of my own suffering came from handing out pieces of myself with no boundaries in place.

That letter wasn't about closure.

It was about clarity.

And lately, the letters aren't always to people.

Sometimes they're to the universe.

Sometimes they're fire-born.

I've started writing down what I want to release—and what I want to receive.

Burning those words with intention.

Saying affirmations during lunar eclipses and new moons.

Paying attention to cycles.

Trusting energy.

Noticing synchronicities.

And you know what?

I'm starting to believe our ancestors had it right.

They listened.

To the sky.

To the soil.

To the silence.

And I'm learning to do the same.

Not because I'm trying to be "spiritual"…

But because I'm finally paying attention to what's already speaking through me.

Chapter 14

The Choice

There's a moment in every journey where the road stops winding and asks for a decision. Not a detour. Not a delay. A decision. For me, that moment came dressed like paperwork:

A Voluntary Early Retirement packet.

A spreadsheet. A benefits breakdown. A question disguised as a form:

Do you stay in the system that no longer feels safe—or do you walk into the unknown?

For over three decades, the federal government was my constant.

It was structure. Stability. Honor.

It gave me a place, a purpose, a paycheck.

But lately, that place feels… fragile.

Like it's turning on the very people who kept it strong.

The promises once made now feel like memories.

And so here I am—at another edge of myself.

For a long time, I believed leaving meant failing.

That retirement was an ending.

That walking away was weakness.

But now I know better.

Sometimes walking away is the most faithful thing you can do.

Not because you're giving up…

but because you've finally stopped clinging to what no longer aligns.

This isn't just about a job.

It's about freedom.

It's about the voice inside me that's been whispering:

"You have more to give—but you can't give it here."

And this time?

I'm listening.

I don't know exactly what's next.

I have ideas. Visions. Possibilities.

But no guarantees.

And yet… I'm not scared.

Because for once, the decision I'm about to make isn't about duty or safety or anyone else's idea of success.

It's about alignment.

It's about truth.

It's about choosing me.

And if I had any doubt—any question about what freedom even felt like—

I was reminded not in an office or a therapy session…

…but on a beach.

Barbados.

Bottom Bay.

A cultural dance exchange with my son's tap group, Northwest Tap.

Just our two families. No crowd. No noise. No pretense.

Just us.

Sitting on the edge of a secluded neighborhood beach,

watching the shadows stretch across the land from the other side of the island,

the sun melting slowly into the water.

There was no script.

No performance.

Just stillness.

That moment?

That was peace.

That was release.

That was freedom.

And if I'm honest, I've had these words with me for years.

I just didn't know how real they'd feel until now:

"I am the master of my fate, I am the captain of my soul."

— William Ernest Henley, "Invictus"

That line has been with me since I pledged Kappa.

Back then, it felt like a challenge.

Now?

It feels like a vow.

And as I look at the path ahead—uncertain but calling—another voice joins it:

"Two roads diverged in a wood, and I— I took the one less traveled by, And that has made all the difference."

— *Robert Frost, "The Road Not Taken"*

This is that moment.

The road.

The difference.

And this time, I'm not choosing from fear.

I'm choosing from freedom.

Epilogue

The Wake-Up Call

When I started this book, I thought I was writing about the past. But as I reach the final page, I realize... I've been writing my present all along.

Because the real test of everything I've learned—everything I've healed—came after I sat down to reflect.

It came in the form of a news headline.

A memo.

A shift in policy from an administration I didn't vote for but still had to live under.

The federal government—the one place that had once symbolized safety, structure, and service—was no longer a sanctuary.

And I?

I was no longer protected.

Remote workers were being forced back into offices.

Job security, once ironclad, was suddenly dangling.

And the writing was on the wall for those of us who had built careers inside systems that no longer valued people over politics.

Then came the notice:

VERA—Voluntary Early Retirement Authority.

An offer.

An out.

A moment of reckoning.

And so the question returned:

Do I stay where I'm safe but stifled?

Or do I leave and finally live?

In the past, I would've delayed.

Prayed.

Asked for permission.

Hoped someone would give me a sign.

But now?

Now I know that when God wants your attention… He doesn't whisper.

He shakes the foundation.

And this—this disruption, this uncertainty—isn't punishment.

It's a wake-up call.

A call to live.

Not obediently.

Not cautiously.

But freely.

Because all of the stories I've shared here—every heartbreak, every spiritual twist, every journaled breakdown, every silent prayer and screaming silence—have led me here:

To this choice.

To this threshold.

To this new, unwritten chapter.

And if you've made it this far, you already know the answer.

You know what I chose.

Because I chose me.

I chose alignment.

I chose faith that doesn't require fear to function.

I chose freedom.

I was always me...

just not a me I wanted to see.

And then I saw my reflection,

and I was not the me I wanted to be.

So I did the work—and only then was I set free.

— DT Comer

About the Author

Dennis T. Comer is a decorated U.S. Army veteran, federal security expert, community leader, and spiritual seeker whose journey spans continents, combat zones, boardrooms, and inner healing. With more than 20 years of military service and another two decades in federal government leadership, Dennis has lived a life of discipline, structure, and service—until life demanded something deeper.

This memoir reflects that calling.

Dennis's reflections in From Hero to Zero to Freedom are rooted in lived experience, not theory—showing how blind obedience, emotional repression, and misplaced trust cost him everything...until he reclaimed his truth. With raw honesty, he shares how trauma, divorce, betrayal, and disillusionment with faith pushed him into spiritual isolation—and how rediscovering his voice, values, and vulnerability set him free.

His latest accomplishment becoming a proud graduate of UCLA's Anderson School of Management (Class of 2025), Dennis continues to build a life driven by integrity, purpose, and freedom. Today, he mentors veterans, supports minority small businesses, and lives by the principle: "You are allowed to outgrow the version of you that others still expect."

Dennis resides in Los Angeles, California, with his wife and son.

www.ingramcontent.com/pod-product-compliance
Lightning Source LLC
Chambersburg PA
CBHW021018090426
42738CB00007B/819